Who Do You THINK You Are?

A Vision Board Workbook for Self-Discovery and Authentic Happiness

———————

Liz Toussaint
The Muniefa Method - Volume 1

Archway Publishing books may be ordered through booksellers or by contacting:

Archway Publishing
1663 Liberty Drive
Bloomington, IN 47403
www.archwaypublishing.com
844-669-3957

Who Do you THINK you are?
A Vision BoardWorkbook for Self-Discovery

Interior Image Credit: Muniefa Abdullah

ISBN: 978-1-6657-5187-2 (sc)
ISBN: 978-1-6657-5188-9 (e)

Library of Congress Control Number: 2023919865

Print information available on the last page.

Archway Publishing rev. date: 11/08/2023

DEDICATION

This book is dedicated to Isa and Laila, my remarkable children, who have graciously allowed me to evolve and heal in their presence. During the times when you may feel lost on your own journeys, my deepest affirmation is that you will discover an inner compass guiding you to your loftiest and most extraordinary self.

Furthermore, I dedicate this book to every weary heart, every relentless achiever, every occasional procrastinator, and every undervalued dreamer. What unites us all is the conditioning of limiting beliefs. As you embark on your quest to figure "it" out, my sincerest affirmation is that you'll uncover a profound comprehension of your heart's true desires. Within this understanding lies the key to a new realm of imaginative possibilities, where you'll effortlessly draw in fresh, delightful experiences that both soothe your soul and invigorate your spirit. I firmly affirm that you will shed all constraints and disempowering beliefs that dare to obstruct your path to deep, soulful breaths and the joyful embrace of each moment, for these "now" moments are deserving of your full attention and gratitude.

ABOUT
"Who Do You THINK You Are?"

This book is cute! Who doesn't love a good vision board experience? However, it's important to understand that this book is not merely an exercise for entertainment. If you are seeking a fun craft, this book may remind you of the less enjoyable aspects of school, and who truly relishes doing homework?

This book is intended for those who are on the path of manifesting, and are looking to gain greater clarity about what they are creating. It's a workbook, requiring you to show up for yourself and be present in your own body. This book is for those who wish to actively shape the person they are becoming while understanding that the journey is all about self-discovery.

If you embark on this transformative journey, by the conclusion of this book, you will attain a newfound sense of clarity, enabling you to connect with and appreciate the pleasures of daily life. Through the practice of mindfulness and presence, you will learn how to tend to your personal well-being by engaging your senses. Your path to self-improvement hinges on recognizing the importance of prioritizing your own needs on your list of daily tasks. As you cultivate a positive state of being, you will naturally attract more fulfilling experiences. This state of harmony resides within your heart and manifests as the calmness found in a deep, soothing breath.

Ultimately, this is a conversation with yourself. Act as your own assistant, be present and show up for yourself.

INTRODUCTION

Hello, I'm Muniefa, my friends call me Liz! I'd like to share a little about myself and the journey that led me to the concept of visualizing through the senses.

I grew up on the south side of Chicago, nestled within a predominantly Black Muslim community. My upbringing was unique, from my point of view - my parents belong to the Silent Generation, my older brothers are Baby Boomers, and I find myself as a child of the late Gen X era. Being the youngest of seven children, I quickly learned the art of transmuting energy. With four brothers and two sisters, each possessing their own distinct needs and quirks, I often felt like I was in everyone's way.

My childhood created a training ground for what would become my greatest challenge: releasing the knee-jerk people-pleasing that I had cultivated to survive in a large family with strong personalities. As I matured and embarked on a path of intentional self-awareness, I began to peel back layers of limiting beliefs and desires that weren't truly my own. My journey into manifestation started, and after years learning to "allow" it became remarkably easy. Creating vision boards with friends and witnessing those visions materialize in reality was undeniably exciting. However, I noticed something crucial was missing – I didn't feel the way I thought I would when I received what I wanted.

Accumulating awards, possessions, and experiences that I once yearned for somehow left me feeling empty. It dawned on me that many of my manifested desires were shaped by trends and external definitions of success. Attaining these goals didn't bring the fulfillment I had envisioned because they were rooted in external perceptions rather than my own authentic desires.

One day, I made a major realization. The things I thought I desperately wanted weren't actually what I desired at all. Instead, I craved the recognition and validation I assumed would come from family and friends once I achieved those goals. This revelation prompted a critical question: What did I truly want? What would genuinely satisfy me? The answer was clear. – satisfaction was a feeling not an object.

Satisfaction felt like freedom – the freedom to be myself, with all my needs met, and love emanating from my very core. This insight was a turning point, but there was a challenge. I had never seen anyone who looked like me, a young black single mother of two from the inner city) truly free. Satisfaction? What is that? Everyone I knew seemed caught in the relentless "rat race," either working for a pension or hustling their talents to make ends meet. So, how could I visualize something I'd never witnessed firsthand?

I began with a deep breathing meditation, turned my focus inward, and explored the desired sensations within my body. What I discovered was that my desires weren't about things; they were about feelings. Since I lacked personal role models for the kind of freedom I sought, I had to rely on my senses to identify and understand this feeling. This process unveiled layers of experiences that allowed me to stay present and recognize when I was truly living the sensations of my desire in real-time. This shift in perspective has enabled me to create and savor some of the most extraordinary experiences in my life. It is my desire that through this workbook, you too can embark on a similar journey, exploring your desires, and manifesting them through the senses to live a life that truly satisfies your soul.

This workbook is a labor of love, born out of my own journey of self-exploration and discovery. I've grappled with questions about my desires, motivations, and the influences that shape my dreams. Through years of introspection and working with countless inspiring individuals, coaches and spiritual advisors and shamans, I've developed a fun method to help untangle these complex threads.

"Do Your Best To Feel Good As Much As You Can!"

- Esther (Abraham) Hicks

Muniefa's MANIFESTO

I believe our collective journey is to be aware of our true selves. Everything else is an exercise to bring us back to us.

I believe humans swim in energy just as fish swim in water. Are fish aware of the ripples they cause in the water? Are humans aware of the ripples they cause in the energy? What happens if a fish is aware of the water? What kind of beautiful ripples would they/you create?

I believe that when you dive deep into the ocean of yourself, you are unaffected by the waves of the surface.

Self Love Pledge:

I pledge allegiance to Myself
and the United Frequencies of my Universe
and to the Collective, who are Aware
One Vibration, under God, indivisible
with Freedom and Self Acceptance for all!

-By Liz Toussaint & Tandaleria Roland

HOW TO USE THIS BOOK

The core truth is that what you feel inside is the only reality. Your ability to be fully present in your body unlocks your superpowers. Being present in each moment, with intention, empowers you to engage in your experiences decisively, either by saying "Yes" or "No" with certainty.

Once you've pinpointed your desired experience, you now have a gauge to steer your decisions. This awareness enables you to identify and gravitate toward experiences aligned with your goals while letting go of those that don't serve your desired outcomes.

Just like most skills, **practice** enhances your confidence. As you practice self-awareness, you develop a deeper connection with your inner voice, fostering greater self-trust, which, in turn, allows you to navigate the world more purposefully.

Begin each page with the first thought that comes to mind. Embrace the boundless possibilities and build upon them as you visualize and create.

When you have reached the list of 10 habits, review the experiences you have visualized on previous pages to inspire an activity that creates and/or supports the sensory experience you would like to have. The goal is to tap into the desired feeling and actively choose to create and participate in those experiences.

Throughout this journey of self-discovery, there's one rule: Trust yourself.

STAY POSITIVE!

Affirmations have become quite popular among those who practice conscious manifestation. When I began crafting affirmations, I used to experience frustration with the results. Often, the outcome would either align exactly with what I said, even if it wasn't what I truly desired, or it would be the opposite of what I wanted.

During a meditation session, I had a profound realization about the power of words. As you work through the affirmations in this book, remember to focus solely on affirming your true desires. Below is the message I received during that meditation:

Imagine the universe as your teacher. When assessing your affirmations or statements, it only acknowledges and credits the positive or descriptive words. Consider the sentence, "I don't want to get a ticket."

In this scenario, the teacher eliminates the word "don't" due to its negative connotation, and it credits you for the remaining portion of the sentence before granting you the experience. So, what experience do you end up receiving? "I want to get a ticket."

Is this the experience you initially desired? Now, consider what happens if you solely affirm the experience you genuinely want. Stay positive! - Muniefa

LEXICON: My Personal Definitions

Affirmative Statement: a sentence that expresses a fact or desired fact, only using positive words

Be: to exist in a specific manner

Become: to transform

Release: is the act of letting go of a behavior, belief or thing for the purpose of relieving oneself from the discomfort associated with it

Journey: is the trip we take on earth from birth to ascendence.

Practice: Doing something repeatedly to get better at it. For instance, practicing a musical instrument, etc. involves intentional repetition to improve your skills

Participate: intentionally engaging

Positive words: These words have forward movement or clearly describe a thing. The word "Discontinue" is a positive word compared to "don't" because "don't" has "no" value. If you sound the word out, it sounds like a closed door. "Discontinue" serves to identify the same as don't, but energetically is an activity of release. "Don't" ends with a cross which signifies a "stop". Discontinue ends with an "e" which flows outward free of resistance

Sizzle: gives a exciting description

WORD INSPIRATION

Below, you'll find a list of words that describe positive feelings. You can use these as sample words to choose from when identifying your emotions and crafting your new world. You can also disregard the categories and use them as you see fit.

FEELINGS	SENSATIONS	ACTIONS	TASTE
Joy	Warmth	Savor	Savory
Gratitude	Plush	Relish	Delicious
Excitement	Fulfillment	Enjoy	Succulent
Inspiration	Freedom	Delight	Exquisite
Safe	Relaxed	Bask	Tantalizing
Confidence	Tranquility	Indulge	Heavenly
Optimism	Lightness	Rejoice	Of God
Bliss	Vitality	Luxuriate	Delightful
Euphoria	Satisfying	Pamper	Yummy
Amazing	Calmness	Celebrate	Mouthwatering
Refreshed	Comfort	Revel	Delectable
Enthusiasm	Cozy	Gratify	Magnificent
Peace	Cushy	Immerse	Decadent

PARTICIPATION AGREEMENT

I, _____, willingly and enthusiastically agree to participate in my own Self-Discovery. I understand and accept the following terms and conditions:

1. **Commitment to Self:** I commit to showing up for myself and engaging wholeheartedly in this self-discovery journey. I understand that self-improvement requires dedication and effort, and I am prepared to invest my time and energy in this process.

2. **Personal Responsibility:** I acknowledge that my progress in this workbook is a reflection of my personal effort and engagement. I take full responsibility for my own growth and development throughout this experience.

3. **Self-Paced Journey:** I recognize that self-discovery is a unique and individual journey. I am encouraged to move at my own pace, allowing myself the time and space I need to explore and reflect on my desires and goals.

4. **Fun and Enjoyment:** I agree to approach this workbook with a positive and open-minded attitude. I understand that the process can be enjoyable and transformative, and I am open to embracing the fun aspects of self-discovery.

5. **Respect for Others:** I will engage with fellow participants, instructors, and coaches with respect and kindness. I understand that we are all on our personal journeys, and I will support others in their growth as they support me in mine.

6. **Confidentiality:** I will respect the confidentiality of others' experiences and insights shared during the program. I will keep private all personal information or insights shared by fellow participants.

7. **Completion of Workbook:** I am committed to completing the workbook exercises and assignments to the best of my ability.

8. **Feedback and Support:** I am open to receiving feedback from instructors, coaches, or peers during this journey. I will actively seek support when needed and offer support to others when appropriate.

By signing this agreement, I affirm that I am dedicated to my own self-discovery, and I am excited about the positive changes and growth that I can facilitate in my life.

Participant's Name: _____ Date _____

Signature: _____

Write a short **draft** bio for yourself based on who you would like to "be" in your life. If a reporter was telling a story about you, what would they say?Use sizzle words and note accomplishments.

_____

_____

_____

_____

_____

_____

_____

_____

_____

_____

_____

_____

_____

_____

_____

_____

_____

_____

_____

_____

ENJOY THE JOURNEY

The assignment is to develop habits that achieve the feeling you believe you would obtain from the goal or thing you desire. Whatever it is that you desire, ask yourself what feeling it will bring, and then determine how you can generate that feeling without actually having met that goal or achieving that thing.

Immersing yourself in the desired feeling attracts the desired outcome. Attracting is what we are constantly doing every moment of every day. While we are always in a state of attraction, at times, our own predefined rules about how our desires should manifest can hinder progress toward our goals. To speed up manifestations, it is best to let go of the "how" and embrace a state of "being." As you progress through this book, you will identify the activities you'd like to pursue. Follow these steps:

1. Ask yourself: What feeling am I expecting to have when I get what I want?
2. Identify the desired feeling
3. Create experiences for yourself that gives you that feeling
4. Create these experiences in small daily habits

Releasing the thought process that hinders your ability to let go and fully immerse yourself in the desired experience creates a sensation of liberation. It's like leaping out of an airplane and embracing the exhilarating free fall then fully taking in the breathtaking landscape. When you're already 30 thousand feet in the air, equipped with protective gear, orientation and support, why go through all that if you're not going to jump and savor the experience? Trying to control the experience may cause you to miss the experience altogether. After all, **you are how you feel.**

Now that you have identified who you THINK you are; write down an experience the person you would like to become would have using an **affirmative statement**:

Example: I am a best-selling Author/Coach

X_____

Add a photo(s), draw a picture or insert a word(s) that represent this description for you

Write one word to describe the overall feeling of this page:

Imagine your desired experience from the previous page has shown up in your life. It is a current reality. **It's the best day of your life, so far.** Tell me all about it!

Describe the experience in detail to the best of your ability.

Have fun!

_____

_____

_____

_____

_____

_____

_____

_____

As you move to the next pages, remember that what you are describing is based on this vision/desire.

Need time to think? Want to color?

1. Where Are You Waking Up?

- Describe the place where you wake up on this ideal day. Is it a cozy bedroom, a cabin in the woods, a beachside bungalow?
- Add a photo(s), draw a picture or insert a word(s) that represents this description for you.

Write one word to describe the overall feeling of this page:

2. **What is the First Scent That Greets You?**

- What aroma fills the air as you begin your day? Is it the scent of fresh coffee, ocean breeze, blooming flowers, or something else?
- Add a photo(s), draw a picture or insert a word(s) that represents this description for you.

Write one word to describe the overall feeling of this page:

3. **Morning Routine: How Does It Unfold?**

- Walk through your morning routine. What activities bring you joy and set a positive tone for the day ahead?
- Add a photo(s), draw a picture or insert a word(s) that represents this description for you.

Write one word to describe the overall feeling of this page:

4. Breakfast Delight: What's on Your Plate?

- Visualize your ideal breakfast. What foods do you see? How do they taste, and what feeling are you experiencing while eating?
- Add a photo(s), draw a picture or insert a word(s) that represents this description for you.

Write one word to describe the overall feeling of this page:

5. Lunchtime: What Are You Eating and With Whom?

- Imagine your lunch. What's on your plate, and who are you sharing it with? Describe the conversations and connections.
- Add a photo(s), draw a picture or insert a word(s) that represents this description for you.

Write one word to describe the overall feeling of this page:

6. Afternoon Adventure: What's Happening?

- Picture your afternoon. Are you exploring new places, trying a new activity, or spending quality time with friends or family?
- Add a photo(s), draw a picture or insert a word(s) that represents this description for you.

Write one word to describe the overall feeling of this page:

7. **Dinner Time: Who's Around the Table?**

- Envision your ideal dinner. Who's present, and what conversations are flowing around the table?

- Describe the setting of your dinner. What's the lighting like? How does the environment contribute to the atmosphere?

- Add a photo(s), draw a picture or insert a word(s) that represents this description for you.

Write one word to describe the overall feeling of this page:

8. **Attire: What Are You Wearing?**
- Detail the outfit you're wearing at each phase of your perfect day. How does it make you feel? What textures and colors are involved?
- Add a photo(s), draw a picture or insert a word(s) that represents this description for you.

Write one word to describe the overall feeling of this page:

9. Evening Wind-Down: How Are You Relaxing?

- Paint a picture of how your evening unfolds. Are you watching a movie, stargazing, reading a book, or engaging in a calming ritual?
- Add a photo(s), draw a picture or insert a word(s) that represents this description for you.

Write one word to describe the overall feeling of this page:

10. Before Sleep: What's the Last Thought?

- As you drift off to sleep, what positive thought or feeling lingers in your mind and body?
- Add a photo(s), draw a picture or insert a word(s) that represents this description for you.

Write one word to describe the overall feeling of this page:

Take a moment to review the previous pages. What are the prominent senses activated?

Write a list of 10 habits that the ideal version of you practices regularly to maintain this sensory experience.

Example: The ideal version of myself is at peace, one of my habits is: Filling my room with my favorite scent as I set the tone before I meditate.

1. _____

2. _____

3. _____

4. _____

5. _____

6. _____

7. _____

8. _____

9. _____

10. _____

Review the list of 10 habits. Compare it to your current life, put a check mark next to the habits you're currently participating in.

What are two (2) habits from the list of 10 that you can start practicing now? How will you easily implement these habits into your current life?

1. _____

_____

_____

_____

2. _____

_____

_____

_____

_____

GRATITUDE

Being in a state of gratitude and appreciation can create an experience of positive energy that attracts more positive energy due to several psychological and emotional factors:

1. **Shift in Focus:** Gratitude and appreciation shift your focus from what you lack or what's going wrong to what you have and what's going right in your life. This change in perspective helps you see the positives more clearly.

2. **Positive Emotions:** Gratitude and appreciation generate positive emotions like joy, contentment, and happiness. These emotions have a direct impact on your overall mood and well-being, leading to a more positive and optimistic outlook.

3. **Neurological Effects**: Studies have shown that practicing gratitude can lead to changes in the brain's neural pathways. It can activate the brain's reward center and the release of dopamine, which is associated with pleasure and reward.

4. **Improved Relationships:** Expressing gratitude and appreciation toward others strengthens social bonds and fosters positive relationships. People are naturally drawn to those who appreciate and value them, leading to more positive social interactions.

5. **Law of Attraction:** The Law of Attraction suggests that positive thoughts and emotions attract positive experiences and outcomes. When you're in a state of gratitude, you emit a positive energy that can attract more positive circumstances and people into your life.

6. **Emotional Contagion:** Your emotions can influence the emotions of those around you. When you express gratitude and appreciation, you spread positivity to others, creating a ripple effect of positive energy.

7. **Increased Awareness:** Gratitude and appreciation require you to become more aware of the present moment and the positive aspects of your life. This heightened awareness allows you to notice and seize opportunities for positivity.

8. **Reduction in Stress:** Gratitude and appreciation have been linked to reduced stress levels. When you're less stressed, you're more likely to attract positive experiences and handle challenges with a clear and positive mindset.

Practicing gratitude and appreciation can create a positive feedback loop. It starts by shifting your focus and generating positive emotions, which then lead to changes in your brain, increased resilience, improved relationships, and a more positive overall outlook. This positive energy, in turn, tends to attract more positive experiences and opportunities into your life.

GRATITUDE INSPIRATION

These sentence starters can be used to express gratitude for a wide range of people, things, experiences, and moments in your life. Feel free to personalize them to fit your specific feelings of appreciation.

Here's a list of gratitude statement starters to help express your appreciation and gratitude:

- I'm so grateful that...
- I truly appreciate when...
- I feel blessed to have...
- I'm thankful for...
- I'm filled with gratitude for...
- My heart sings when...
- I cherish...
- I'm so pleased that...
- It warms my heart to know...
- I count my blessings every day for...
- I'm deeply appreciative of...
- I'm touched by...
- I'm so glad to have the gift of...
- I'm appreciative of the small things, like...
- I'm grateful for the love and support of...
- I'm thankful for the lessons I've learned from...
- I'm thankful for the abundance of...

NEXT STEPS

Congratulations! If you've entered answers into every page up to this point, you have a considerable amount of information around your desires.

Periodically review what you have identified. If something changes, make the necessary adjustments. If you want to add something, feel free to do so. Keep these experiences and items you enjoy in mind.

The focus over the next 10 weeks is to practice acknowledging, when you encounter something from this book while living your life.

Pause and appreciate its presence in your experience. Acknowledging and appreciating it will enhance your overall experience and invite more similar experiences.

For the next 10 weeks select one experience from this list to actively participate in on a routine basis. At the beginning of each month, with your desired experience in mind, create an affirmation that supports it. For example:

I described waking up near water, feeling relaxed while eating fruit and reading a book. My affirmation for that experience is: 'I am thankful to wake up in such a wonderful space!' I acknowledge that my current place IS wonderful, and I allow myself to feel relaxed, eat fruit and read a book in my current experience.

For 10 weeks, record a weekly statement of gratitude at the beginning of each week and recite it each day to keep yourself focused and motivated.

1. _____

2. _____

3. _____

4. _____

5. _____

6. _____

7. _____

8. _____

9. _____

10. _____

PLAYLIST:

Music is the best subconscious vibration influencer. What are your go- to sounds, talks, or songs that play in the "energetic space" you want to be in? Use this log as a guide to help maintain your desired experience, and remind yourself who you think you are!

Desired Feeling	Song/Audio
Ex: At Peace	Breath it in by Beautiful Chorus
Empowered	
Loved	
Grateful	
Excited	

Week 11

Describe what you are enjoying in your life experience now:

_____

_____

_____

_____

_____

_____

_____

_____

Printed in the United States
by Baker & Taylor Publisher Services